Tomahawk I/II Combat Log

European Theatre

1941-42

Hugh Harkins

ISBN: 1-903630-49-5
ISBN-13: 978-1-903630-49-5

Tomahawk I/II
Combat Log

© Hugh Harkins 2014

Published by Centurion Publishing
United Kingdom

ISBN 10: 1-903630-49-5
ISBN 13: 978-1-903630-49-5

This volume first published 2014

Cover design © Centurion Publishing & Createspace

Page layout, concept and design © Centurion Publishing

The Publisher and Author would like to thank all organisations and services for
their assistance and contributions in the preparation of this volume

CONTENTS

INTRODUCTION

The purpose of this volume is to provide a comprehensive detailed study of the operational and combat operations of the RAF's Curtiss Tomahawk MK.I/IIA fighter aircraft which were employed operationally in the European Theatre, commencing with air defence patrols in May 1941 with No.403 RCAF Squadron. Found wanting in performance at high and medium altitudes, the Tomahawk was very quickly replaced in the fighter/interceptor role by Supermarine Spitfires from the end of May 1941, the same month that No.403 Squadron had become operational on Tomahawks.

The main phase of Tomahawk operations in the European Theatre commenced on 16 October 1941 when No.26 Squadron commenced Rhubarb operations over Northern France. Several other squadrons conducted Rhubarbs over France and the Low Countries from late 1941 until January 1942, and No.268 Squadron flew Rhubarbs and fighter escort operations.

A brief description of the genesis and development of the Tomahawk fighter is laid down, but the volume is not designed to be a comprehensive monograph on that subject. The volume is copiously supported by a wealth of operational documents including Squadron Composite Rhubarb Reports; Squadron Operational Records and pilot reports, some of which are reproduced verbatim. Operational documents have been tied up against German reports whenever possible.

1

CURTISS TOMAHAWK I/II

Curtiss Tomahawk and Kittyhawk fighters were operated extensively by the British RAF (Royal Air Force) and Commonwealth air forces during the Second World War, particularly in the Middle and Far East. However, Tomahawk I/IIA fighters were also operated in the European Theatre, by British and Canadian squadron based in Britain, flying a myriad of operational missions ranging from standing air patrols, interception scrambles, convoy protection, fighter escort and Rhubarb and Popular missions over Northern France.

Tomahawk was the British name applied to Curtiss Model 81 fighters taken over from French orders and others that were direct British purchases. The aircraft was generally similar to the USAAC (United States Army Air Corp) P-40B Pursuit Fighter. The P-40 was itself developed from the Curtiss P-36, designed in 1935, the 10th production example of which was converted to act as the prototype XP-40. By the time the P-36 was flying it had become clear that it was vastly inferior to the latest generation of European designed fighter aircraft, particularly in high altitude performance and armament. Attempts to improve performance led to the XP-37 which accommodated a turbo supercharged Allison V-1710-11 inline, liquid cooled engine. Although an improvement over the P-36A, the new aircraft proved disappointing and the engine proved to be extremely unreliable.

The design team, under Dr. Donavan R Berlin, went back to the drawing board and came up with another design, designated XP-40, in 1938; the P-36 being converted to the XP-40 which was powered by an Allison V-1710-19. This aircraft conducted its maiden flight as the XP-40 on 14 October 1938. After evaluations of the XP-40 and other fighter designs the USAAC ordered modifications to be incorporated and the aircraft was selected for production, with 540 ordered. These early P-40's, production of which commenced in 1940, were armed with 2 x 0.50 in Browning machine guns in the nose and 2 x 0.30 in Brownings in each wing.

The Curtiss XP-40 (above) was developed from the XP-67 which was itself developed from the Curtiss P-36A (top). The most notable difference was the switch from the radial to the inline engine. USAF

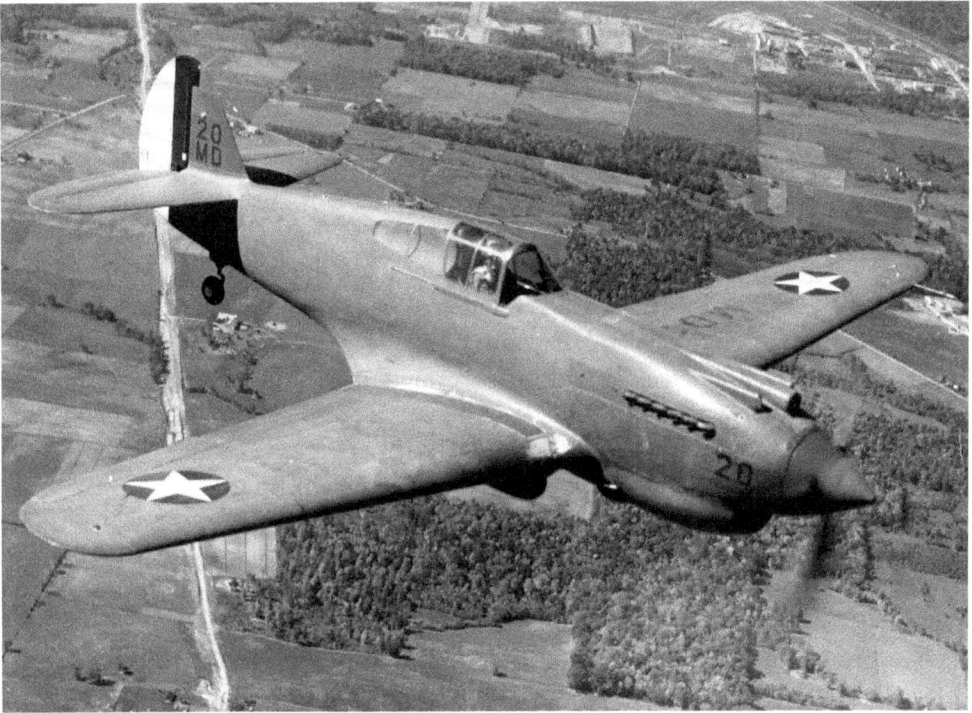

During the course of 1941 the P-40 was being installed as the standard fighter aircraft in USAAC service, remaining so until well into 1943. USAF

The P-40 is often described as being obsolete by European standards by the time of its first flight in October 1938. While there is no doubt that it was outclassed by the best European fighters then in service such as the Supermarine Spitfire I and Messerschmitt Me.109E, and even more so by European fighters being designed, such as the German Focke Wulf FW.190, the P-40 had adequate performance compared to many other fighters then in service. For the RAF, which would adopt the aircraft mainly for the Army Co-Operation role; the type being quickly rejected for the fighter role after a few weeks of operational flying, the Tomahawk I/II models were a significant improvement on the Westland Lysander that it would augment and partially replace. The Lysander itself could be described as a utility aircraft with a light bombing capability, whereas the Tomahawk would allow operations to be carried out over contested airspace such as Northern France; areas that were out of bounds for the slow flying Lysander's during daylight hours.

France had ordered the Curtiss Model 81 and the first of these was ready by April 1940. When France accepted German terms for an Armistice in June 1940 the French order was in limbo, but was soon taken over by Britain which designated the aircraft Tomahawk I. French orders for the Curtiss Model 87 were also taken over by Britain, these aircraft being known in Britain as Kittyhawk, a type which would go on to serve Commonwealth Air Forces in a number of theatres.

As can be best deciphered from contradictory manufacturing and customer records, Britain ordered 1,180 Curtiss Model 81's as direct purchases; these aircraft being named Tomahawk. Records show that 10 USAAC P-40C's were also received by Britain, but these aircraft appear not to have been allocated British serials. One hundred and forty Curtiss Model H81-A's were delivered as Tomahawk I's. These were basically equivalent to the USAAC P-40B, armed with four wing mounted 0.3 in Browning machine guns. These aircraft were allocated serials AH741-AH840 and AH841/AH880. It is often falsely stated that these aircraft were deemed unsuitable for combat and quickly relegated to a training only role by the RAF. However, many of these aircraft were allocated to squadrons and were used on Rhubarb operations over France from 16 October 1941 until 22 January 1942.

The Tomahawk IIA, 110 aircraft covered by serials AH881-AH990, introduced improvements, including armour protection and self-sealing fuel tanks; twenty three were sent o the Soviet Union and one went to Canada.

The Tomahawk IIB designation covered 930 aircraft equivalent to the USAAC P-40C. This model was used to equip RAF, RAAF and SAAF squadrons operating in the Middle East and North Africa from June 1941 and 100 were transferred to China for use by the AVG (American Volunteer Group). A further 23 were transferred to the Soviet Union and small numbers went to Turkey and Egypt. British serials allocated to the four Tomahawk IIB production blocks consisted of AL199-AL999 and AK100-AK570.

Top: The Tomahawk's career as an operational fighter with home based squadrons was relatively short lived, with only the MK.I and MK.IIA being used operationally; MK.IIB's being used operationally in other theatres, notably the Middle East. This aircraft, AH926, is a Tomahawk IIA. RAF Above: Tomahawk IIB's were employed by a number of Home Based units non-operationally. This MK.IIB, AK184, is at Air Service Training Ltd at Hamble, Hampshire. It later went to the RAE at Farnborough, remaining in service until 1944. MAP

Cockpit of Tomahawk IIB, AK184, at Air Service Training Ltd, Hamble, Hampshire. The cockpit of the IIB differed little from the cockpit of the MK.I/IIA. MAP

Following the crisis and intense battles of 1940, culminating in the Battle of Britain, which continued into the winter months, the British and Commonwealth forces stationed in Britain continued a program of build up and re-equipments. The Westland Lysander's, which had been a mainstay of Army Co-Operation Squadrons, had been shown to be completely inadequate during the German conquest of France and the Low Countries in May and June 1940. Re-equipment became possible with deliveries of Curtiss Tomahawk I/IIA fighters taken over from French contracts and British direct purchases. While the Tomahawk was inferior to the first line fighter aircraft in RAF service at the time, it was considered adequate for the Army Co-Operation role as a partial replacement for the Lysander.

Although the Tomahawk was outclassed by the best of the European fighter aircraft such as the Spitfire, Me.109 and FW.190, and was considered to be obsolete in many respects even before its first flight, in many respects it had adequate performance for operations at the lower altitudes associated with the Army Co-Operation role, being reasonably manoeuvrable and possessing reasonable speed. Maximum speed was 347 mph, while the Spitfire V variants were typically around 374 mph. Climb rate of the Spitfire V was also much superior to that of the Tomahawk; the superiority increasing further at heights above 20,000 ft. However, the Tomahawk was in every respect a fighter aircraft whose high performance, compared to the lumbering Lysander, would allow some squadrons to participate in Rhubarb operations over German occupied Europe, something which the Lysander was simply too vulnerable to accomplish.

No Tomahawk IIB's were used operationally by the home based Squadrons, but Tomahawk I and IIA's were used operationally by four squadrons. Although no less than 12 squadrons would equip with Tomahawk I/II's in the Army Co-Operation role in the European theatre, the first squadron to become operational on the type was No.403 RCAF (Royal Canadian Air Force) Squadron which operated the aircraft in the traditional fighter role, albeit very briefly, prior to reequipping with Supermarine Spitfires.

No.26, No.268 Squadrons and No.400 RCAF Squadron operated Tomahawks in the Army Co-Operation role. No.26 Squadron flew a number of Rhubarbs offensive operations over France from 16 October 1941 until 22 January 1942. During the course of these operations 26 Squadron had several engagements with Luftwaffe Me.109F fighters. From October 1941 No.268 Squadron operated Tomahawks on Rhubarbs over France and Holland and in early 1942 flew mixed convoy protection patrols with Fighter Command Spitfires. No.400 Squadron commenced operations in November 1941, flying Rhubarb and Popular operations over France until 5 January 1942. The operational squadrons suffered a number of Tomahawks lost or damaged as a result of enemy fighters, ground fire, accidents and friendly fire.

2

403 SQUADRON RCAF TOMAHAWK OPERATIONS - FIGHTER COMMAND SUMMER 1941

No.403 Squadron RCAF was the only home based squadron equipped with Curtiss Tomahawks to become operational with Fighter Command. Formed at RAF Baginton, Coventry, on 1 March 1941, the squadron, which was the first of the RCAF overseas formed squadrons under the BCATP (British Commonwealth Air Training Plan), was equipped with Tomahawk I/IIA. However, the unsuitability of the Tomahawk for the fighter role saw this type replaced by Supermarine Spitfires after a short period of operations with Tomahawks.

Throughout March and early April 1941 the squadron prepared for Tomahawk operations. On 7 April, a Fairey Battle and a Miles Magister took two spare pilots to Eastleigh where two Tomahawks were collected and flown to Baginton – the squadron had previously received one or two Tomahawks for training. The following day a Lysander flew to Eastleigh with a pilot who collected another Tomahawk. On the 9th, two Tomahawks were flown to Eastleigh for modifications, the pilots returning in two other Tomahawks. On the 10th a Tomahawk was slightly damaged when a bullet went through the prop while the guns were being tested at the butts. This problem would plague all Tomahawk squadrons over the coming months, on the butts and in air firing.

Coventry suffered a heavy air raid during the night of 8/9 April and Coventry and Birmingham were raided on the night of 9/10 April. On the night of 10/11 April Coventry was raided for the third straight night, this time nine bombs falling on Baginton aerodrome near to the dispersal area.

On the 17th a Tomahawk was damaged when the pilot force landed the aircraft in a field close to Elmdon airfield, Birmingham. The following day another Tomahawk force landed at Bassingbourn, the aircraft suffering slight damage. Accidents continued to plague the squadron when on 28 April three

Tomahawks were damaged, the circumstances best told in the words of the squadron diary. "First member, Sgt. Morrison, overshot on landing at Baginton, hit a gun post and damaged starboard wing and undercarriage. The second member, P/O Anthony, also overshot but improved on first performance by colliding with another Tomahawk and mounting his machine on top of it. The result being slightly suggestive and a rumour has now got about that production of Aircraft is now being speeded up by breading."

These are the first Tomahawks I/IIA's to enter operational service with the RAF. The aircraft are operating with No.403 Squadron RCAF at RAF Baginton, Warwickshire. RAF

A Tomahawk was lost on 30 April when the aircraft went into a spin during a "battle climb"; the pilot, Sgt. Tomlinson, baling out, landing with nothing more serious than a slight concussion.

The squadron received three more Tomahawks, which were collected from Lossiemouth on 5 May, but accidents continued with Tomahawk AH879, flown by Sgt. Morrison, crashing while landing at Baginton on 7 May.

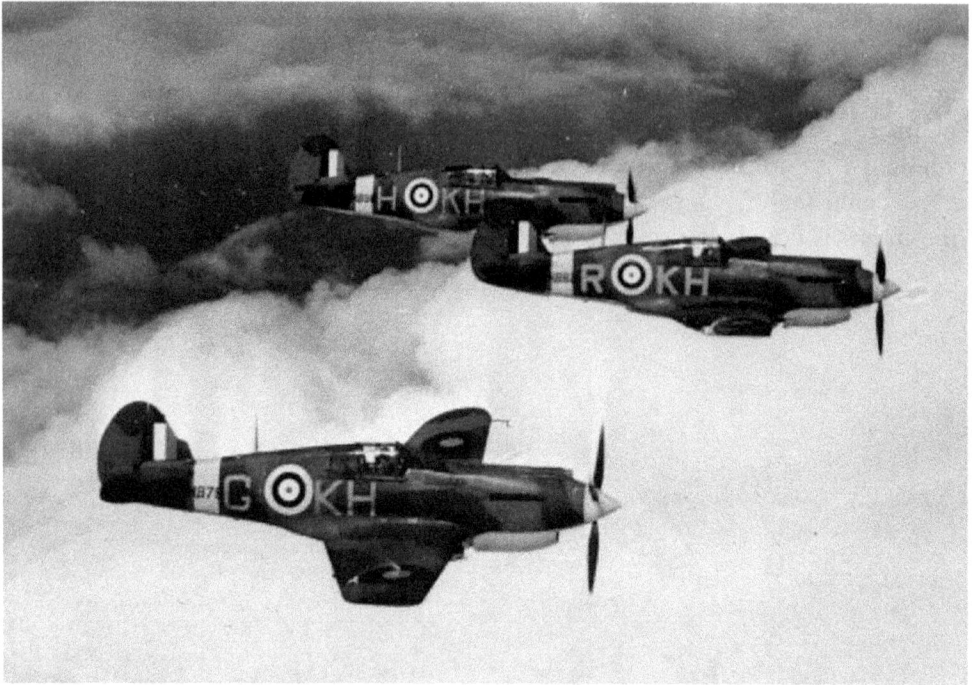

Three Tomahawks from No.403 RCAF Squadron during a training flight in 1941. The aircraft nearest is a Tomahawk I, AH878/KH-G, whilst the other two are Tomahawk IIA's, AH896/KH-H and AH882/KH-R. RAF

403 Squadron was declared operational on 11 May 1942, and, with moderately fair weather, a patrol was conducted at 25,000 ft by two Tomahawks flown by S/Ldr. Morris and P/O Anthony; the aircraft taking off at 13.30 hours and landing at 14.10 hours. At 14.40 three Tomahawks, flown by F/Lt. Gillen, P/O Ford and Sgt. Sones, took off for firing practice but were detailed to intercept a suspected enemy raider. They failed to make an interception, F/Lt. Gillen claiming that he spotted a smoke trail from an aircraft. The Section landed at 15.30 hours.

12.5.1941: Two Tomahawks took off on patrol at 11.00 hours; the patrol being conducted at 15,000 ft over the base as an enemy aircraft had been plotted in the vicinity at that altitude. The Tomahawks failed to intercept and landed at 12.15 hours. Another Section of two Tomahawks took off at 11.40 hours with the same instructions as the first section; patrol the base at 15,000 ft, landing at 12.20.

14.5.1941: Weather conditions were poor with a cloud base down to 800 ft. Two Tomahawks took off at 14.10 hours to patrol over Baginton at the height of the cloud base, one aircraft landing at 14.20 and the other landing at 14.40.

17.5.1941: Between 15.40 and 16.40 hours No.403 Squadron maintained a patrol of Tomahawks (undisclosed number) over Lichfield at an altitude of 20,000 ft as an enemy aircraft had been reported operating in the area; nothing, however, was encountered.

21.5.1941: Two Tomahawks took off at 19.00 hours to patrol over base at an altitude of 10,000 ft. No enemy aircraft were encountered and the patrol landed at 19.35 hours. Two Tomahawks from 'B' Flight took off at 21.10 hours. The aircraft were ordered, by mistake, to patrol the base below the cloud base, whereas they were actually supposed to be on a training flight tasked with a practice interception of paratroops being dropped on the airfield as part of an exercise. The aircraft landed at 21.20.

On this date a Lt. Zemke from the USAAC was attached to the squadron as an official observer for "the US government".

24.5.1941: Three Tomahawks took off at 15.45 hours with orders to patrol base at 10,000 ft, landing at 16.45 after an uneventful patrol. Two Tomahawks took off to patrol the base at 18.20, landing at 18.30.

25.5.1941: Two Tomahawks took off at 12.25 hours to patrol the base at 8,000 ft. One of the pilots, Sgt. Sones, reported that he thought he saw a smoke trail from an aircraft at an altitude of 20,000 ft. The Tomahawks were unable to intercept and landed at 13.15 hours. Two more Tomahawks had taken off on patrol at 12.30; landing at 13.35 hours.

27.5.1941: Two Tomahawks took off at 14.05 hours to patrol Kidderminster at 10,000 ft. These aircraft landed at 15.35, no enemy aircraft having been encountered.

On the 28th, 403 Squadron began flying Spitfires on training flights for the first time; both flights operating with their new aircraft. There were two patrols of two aircraft, the first taking off at 13.30 to patrol Leamington, landing at 14.50; the second took off at 16.30 to patrol Worcester, landing at 17.15. Squadron records are incomplete with no Form 541. The available records do not state which type of aircraft was used for these patrols, Tomahawk or Spitfire. What was clear was that the squadrons days as a Tomahawk Squadron were numbered; a move to Ternhill commencing on 30 May; nine Spitfires and six Tomahawks departing for Ternhill on the 31st; 403 now effectively a Spitfire squadron.

3

26 ARMY CO-OPERATION SQUADRON TOMAHAWK OPERATIONS –RHUBARBS OVER FRANCE

From 1 July 1940, No.26 Squadron came under the orders of XII Corp (3, 45 and 1 (London) Divisions). Its anti-invasion role was laid down as tactical reconnaissance by day within the Corp area, and not extending beyond the beach. In addition, the Squadron was required to bomb in exceptional circumstances, e.g. when an invading force was approaching the coast or was in the process of disembarking. For the bombing role the Lysander's would carry two x 120 lb GP bombs and ten 20 lb bombs. Of course, the invasion never came and the squadron was not called on.

At 21 April 1941 No.26 Squadron had nine Tomahawks' on strength at Gatwick; another two aircraft allocated to the squadron were at Duxford engaged in trials, bringing to 11 the total strength. The squadron also had 11 Lysander's, nine of which were "ready for disposal" and two others which the squadron put in a request to retain as target drogue towing aircraft and for conducting "photographic demands" for XII Corp.

The Squadron continued working up on the Tomahawk and conducting training exercises with the Army, building up confidence in the Tomahawk aircraft as it prepared to commence Rhubarb operations over France, the first of which was conducted on 16 October 1941.

16.10.41: Two Tomahawks flown by W/Cdr. Butler and F/O Fleming took off from Manston at 16.14 hours tasked with photographing the beaches in the Le Touquet – Berck area. The aircraft reached the French coast, receiving some "heavy but inaccurate flak from Foucamp area". Cloud cover was 10/10ths at sea level with rain and generally bad visibility over the Channel, resulting in the Tomahawks abandoning the task; turning back when off Hardelot, landing at Manston at 16.55 hours.

No.26 Squadron, based at Gatwick, Sussex, was the most operationally active of the home based Tomahawk squadrons, employing the type on Rhubarb (offensive photographic reconnaissance) operations over France from 16 October 1941 until 22 January 1942. The two aircraft nearest the camera, AH896/RM-Y and AH893/RM-D, are Tomahawk MK IIA's whilst the aircraft furthest from the camera, AH791/RM-E, is a MK.I. All three of these aircraft conducted Rhubarb operations over France in late 1941; AH791 being damaged when it force landed after an abortive Rhubarb on 21 November. RAF

Two Tomahawks flown by F/O Dawson and P/O Baring departed Manston at 16.20 for a Rhubarb operation in the Le Touquet area. Adverse weather forced one aircraft to abort when about 3 miles off the coast between Cap Griz Nez and Berck. This aircraft returned and landed at Manston at 17.05 hours. The other Tomahawk crossed the French coast about five miles south of Boulogne at an altitude of 2,000 ft, returning to the coast on a reciprocal course when the pilot saw what he described as "two soldiers carrying a large black box on beach". He opened fire and "knocked them down" then flew about 3 miles out to sea before returning and noting the soldiers "lying motionless by box". The Tomahawk landed back at Manston at 17.30 hours after an inauspicious start to the squadrons Rhubarb operations.

17.10.41: Two Tomahawks flown by W/Cdr. Butler and F/O Fleming took off from Manston at 10.09 hours to photograph the beaches in the Le Touquet - Berck area. The aircraft flew towards France and then down the coast at a distance of 5 miles out to sea from Cap Griz Nez to Le Touquet at which point the mission was abandoned due to "lack of cloud". Cloud cover had been 4/10ths at 8,000 ft with improving conditions to the west. The Tomahawks landed back at Manston at 10.46 am.

18.10.41: Two Tomahawks flown by F/Lt. Goodale and P/O Baird departed Manston at 13.09 hours to photograph beaches in the Le Touquet – Berck area. The aircraft left the English coast behind at Dungeness and crossed the French coast at Berck at 0 ft, following which the aircraft split formation; one flying inland to the north about 2 miles where it attacked a "suspected" gun position on the beach area some 2 miles to the north of Berck Plage. The pilot reported that the "gun crew of six fell to the ground, but gun not seen on account of camouflage". The Tomahawk then flew seaward before returning and re-crossing the coast at Merlimont Plage, and then flew north for 4 miles, returning home and landing at Manston at 14.09 hours.

The second Tomahawk strafed "three officers entering hotel at Berck" flew to the area of Berck aerodrome where no activity was reported. The aircraft then strafed some huts seen in a wood about one and a quarter miles east of Berck aerodrome, then flew out north of Merlimont, opening fire on a lorry described as carrying troops; results of the attack not being observed. The aircraft took a few photographs during the mission and returned, landing at Manston at 14.04 hours.

At 15.50 hours 2 Tomahawks flown by F/O Rhind and F/O Dawson took off from Manston on a Rhubarb over the Le Touquet area. The two aircraft crossed the French coast about three miles south of Le Touquet before turning south at the railway. A goods train with covered wagons was observed in a railway station, thought to be Rang de Flier, and this was strafed. Following this attack the Tomahawks separated; one heading southward to Waben where it strafed a "staff car" making three passes. This aircraft then attacked a searchlight post on the north bank of the river Authie, about a mile from the mouth of the river. Following the attack, the results of which were not observed, the aircraft returned to Manston where it landed at 16.57 hours.

The second Tomahawk, after separating, flew south towards the river Authie which it followed, exiting out by the estuary. It strafed a machine gun post on the south bank of the river with unobserved results; no return fire being noted. The aircraft then re-crossed the Channel, visibility being down to 1,000 yards with intermittent rain, the aircraft landing at Manston at 17.03 hours.

19.10.41: Two Tomahawks flown by S/Ldr. Hadfield and F/O Bluett took off from Manston at 11.54 hours on a Rhubarb operation of the Montreuil area. The Tomahawks crossed the cost into the Channel at Dungeness and when off Berck, France, they turned south towards Dieppe due to a lack of cloud cover in the Berck area. Conditions to the south were found to be more favourable and the Tomahawks crossed the coast at St Valery at which point they separated. The first aircraft flew east and strafed hangers on an aerodrome thought to be Dieppe St Aubin. No aircraft were noted on the ground and there was apparently no return fire. The pilot continued and noted "about 250 goods trucks… in sidings three miles south of Dieppe", the aircraft being subjected to light flak from the Dieppe area, the pilot diving under H.T. Cables to escape, exiting some three miles east of Dieppe before returning home to land at Manston at 13.07.

The second aircraft, on separating, flew inland for around five miles before turning east for about five more miles. Nothing of importance was noted and on its way out the aircraft strafed "three light A.A. M.G. posts", about 2 miles west of St Valery. Return fire was noted and results of attack were unobserved. This aircraft landed at Manston at 13.20.

25.10.41: Two Tomahawks flown by S/Ldr. Hadfield and P/O Baird took off from Gatwick at 10.25 hours on a Rhubarb operation in the Le Touquet area of France. The aircraft crossed into the Channel from Dungeness at 10.45, but the mission was aborted when about five miles out from the coast due to a lack of cloud cover. The Tomahawks landed at Manston at 11.29 hours.

27.10.41: Two Tomahawks flown by F/Lt. Wheller and F/O Greville took off from Gatwick at 10.35 for a Rhubarb operation. The English coast was crossed at Dungeness and the aircraft flew on course for Berck, France, but the mission was aborted ten miles out from the coast due to a thick haze and the aircraft subsequently landed at Manston at 11.35 hours.

28.10.41: At 10.28 hours two Tomahawks flown by F/Lt. Wheller and F/O Greville took off from Gatwick on a Rhubarb. They crossed the English coast at Ramsgate at 10.35 and crossed on the Continental side near Coxyde Bains at 10.50 hours. The aircraft turned south going round Furnes. Continuing they crossed over a railway somewhere between Nieuport and Dixmude, then turned back to Coxyde, one of the aircraft strafing a gun post about half a mile west of Coxyde Bains with unobserved results. Photographs were taken of Coxyde aerodrome which was noted to have a "large number of workmen", and a hospital near Coxyde Bains was also photographed. At Furnes a barge was noted to be under construction with a further five or six noted in the canal. The aircraft attempted to photograph the coast west of Coxyde but they were "driven off by heavy M.G. firing tracer". Cloud over target areas was 10/10ths at 1,000 ft with visibility of 6/8 miles. Both aircraft returned and landed at Gatwick at 11.40 hours.

Details are recorded on a film magazine removed from the Type F.24 aerial camera port of a No.26 Squadron Tomahawk I after it landed at Gatwick, Sussex, following a training flight over England. The airmen write down the aircraft serial number, date and time before the film was transferred to a Mobile Darkroom at Gatwick where it was processed.

A second operation was flown in the afternoon; two Tomahawks flown by F/O Corbett-Wilson and P/O Baird taking off from Gatwick at 14.30 hours on a reconnaissance of the Dunkirk area. The aircraft crossed from Ramsgate at 14.55, crossing the French coast two miles west of Dunkirk at 15.15 hours. There was no wire noted on the beaches, but several machine gun posts were noted in the dunes. One of the Tomahawks strafed a goods train one mile south west of Dunkirk with unobserved results. Both aircraft then conducted a reconnaissance of the canal between Dunkirk and Herques (probably Arques), no barges being located. It was noted that "All flat fields had tripod obstructions about 10ft high". The Tomahawks then turned west and re-crossed the railway near Loon Plage, one aircraft then strafing a goods train consisting of 15 closed trucks; the train being seen to stop "in clouds of steam". The aircraft re-crossed the coast west of Le Clipon at 15.35; an unoccupied machine gun post being noted, but no wire. The Tomahawks returned home, landing at Gatwick at 16.00 hours.

Tomahawk I AH791/RM-E in flight in 1941. This aircraft was extensively used on Rhubarb operations over France, particularly during October and November 1941. RAF

30.10.41: Four Tomahawks flown by W/Cdr. Butler, F/O Fleming, P/O Dawson and P/O Baird flew to Manston from where they were to fly a "Cross Channel long-range gun ranging" operation to spot fall of shot for Royal Marine 14" Siege Guns firing across the Channel. This operation was cancelled due to unsuitable weather conditions. Two of the Tomahawks, flown by F/O Dawson and P/O Baird, took off at 16.38 hours to fly a Rhubarb over the Dunkirk area.

The Composite Rhubarb Report for this operation is reproduced below verbatim:

6 AIR LIAISON SECTION

No. 26 A.C. Squadron, R.A.F.
APPENDIX "L" TO WAR DIARY, OCT, 1941.

30 October, 1941. Two Tomahawks, F/O Dawson and P/O Baird left MANSTON 16.38 hrs. on RHUBARB, DUNKIRK area. Crossed coast 1 mile WEST of DUNKIRK at 0 ft. where aircraft separated. Aircraft "A" attacked convoy of four or five large lorries at ST. POL-SUR-MER. All vehicles halted. Orbited and recrossed coast EAST of DUNKIRK/MARDYCK Aerodrome. Intense light FLAK. Convoy four or five large vessels largest about 2000 tons sighted 1 -2 miles off GRAVELINES proceeding WEST at 17.00 hours. Immediately returned to base to report. Aircraft "B" attacked one of three M.G. posts on coast one mile WEST of DUNKIRK, no return fire. Flew SOUTH and attacked four barges moored in canal DE BOURBOURG. Barges seen hit. Flew SOUTH to CANAL DE LA COLME – no movement seen. Turned N.W. and made three attacks on about fifteen barges in CAN DE BOURBOURG about two miles EAST of BOURBOURG. Barges seen to be hit. At conclusion of attack bullets seen entering port wing and M.E.109 passed under aircraft. Own aircraft gave and got in one long burst before losing enemy aircraft in intense FLAK over GRAVELINES. Photos taken. Aircraft landed MANSTON 17.25 hours. 10/10ths cloud 1000 ft. in DUNKIRK Area visibility 1 mile in rain. Fine to NORTH and East and cloud 9/10ths 2000 ft. at GRAVELINES. F/O DAWSON slightly injured.

1.11.41: Three Tomahawks, AH898 (F/Lt. Wheller), AH770 (F/Lt. Goodale) and AH755 (F/O Dawson), took off from Manston at 14.40 hours to conduct an offensive Photographic Reconnaissance) of the St. Josse – Samer – Dannes areas. When two miles out from Dungeness one of the aircraft was forced to abort due to oil trouble. This aircraft landed back at Manston at 15.05 hours. The other two Tomahawks continued towards the French coast, but aborted the mission when about 5 miles off Berck due to lack of cloud cover, which was about 1/10ths at 1,000 ft and 3/10ths at 6,000/8,000 ft in the Boulogne area. The two Tomahawks returned to Manston, landing at 15.25 hours.

2.11.41: Two Tomahawks, AH791 (F/Lt. Rhind) and AH755 (F/O Dawson), took off from Manston at 15.55 hours to photograph a factory at St. Josse and a Transformer Station at Tigery to assess bomb damage. The mission's secondary task was to photograph the beaches in the Le Touquet – Berck area. The Tomahawks crossed over water at Dungeness at 16.05 and crossed the French coast half a mile south of Merlimont Plage at 16.22, following which the aircraft separated. Tomahawk AH791 (F/Lt. Rhind) flew east towards St Josse to where it was noted that the most northerly of the two factories to the east of the railway had been "badly damaged". The pilot then flew north to photograph the transformer station at Tigery which was noted to have been only slightly damaged. Following the photograph runs AH791 flew to Curly Station where it strafed goods trucks. The aircraft then crossed about a quarter of a mile north of the village of Hardelot where it was subjected to some light anti-aircraft fire.

After separating, Tomahawk AH755 few to the north side of Berck aerodrome where it strafed some huts, receiving anti-aircraft return fire. The pilot observed a pair of Me.109's taking off and heading south east; other fighters being noted in dispersal bays. Leaving Berck, the Tomahawk was flown across Le Bout d' Airon aerodrome where aircraft were strafed on the ground. These aircraft, which immediately collapsed, were thought to be dummy's used as decoys. The aircraft then flew over Merlimont Plage where it was subjected to light anti-aircraft fire from a tower located in the village. A machine gun post in the sand dunes south of Merlimont was strafed; no return fire being noted. Over the target areas cloud cover had been 9/10^{ths} at 2,000 ft, with 10/10^{ths} at 1,000 ft over the Channel, with heavy rain. Both Tomahawks landed at Manston at 17.00 hours.

Tomahawk IIA AH896 of No.26 Squadron in 1941. RAF

3.11.41: Two Tomahawks, AH857 (F/O Fleming) and AH755 (P/O Baird), took off from Manson at 14.22 hours with the primary task of photographing the beaches in the Le Touquet – Berck area and Berck aerodrome. The aircraft crossed over water at Dungeness at 14.35, but when mid-Channel the mission was aborted due to unfavourable weather. The aircraft returned to Manston, landing at 14.50.

4.11.41: Three Tomahawks, AH887 (W/Cdr. Butler), AH857 (F/O Fleming) and AH755 (P/O Baird), took off from Manston at 13.02 hours on an offensive photographic reconnaissance of Le Touquet aerodrome and beaches, supporting a low level Ramrod operation by No.607 Squadron Hurricanes.

The Composite Rhubarb Report for his operation is reproduced below verbatim:

6 AIR LIAISON SECTION

No. 26 A.C. Squadron, R.A.F.
APPENDIX "D" TO WAR DIARY, NOVEMBER, 1941.

Composite "RHUBARB" Report.

Three Tomahawks, W/Cmdr. Butler, F/O. Fleming and P/O. Baird left MANSTON, 13.02 hours, 4.11.41 on offensive Photo/Recce of LE TOUQUET aerodrome and beaches. Operations were carried out in conjunction with low ramrod attack on LE TOUQUET aerodrome by 607 Squadron. Crossed coast at 500 feet at MERLIMONT PLAGE from where light Flak was encountered from tower. Aircraft separated. W/Cmdr. Butler turned NORTH at railway and saw two Hurricanes drop bombs on railway line which is thought to have been hit. Photos taken. Turned WEST at ETAPLES. Considerable light Flak from NORTH side of estuary. Machine gunned hanger and huts on WEST side of aerodrome. Hits observed. Came out SOUTH of LE TOUQUET. F/O. Fleming encountered Flak from a gun position at ST. JOSSE and turned NORTH to river CANCHE. Crossed LE TOUQUET aerodrome at 600 feet and observed bombs from Hurricanes falling on dispersal areas on WEST and N.W. sides. Photos taken. Flew out over town and fishing fleet observed in estuary. P/O Bairs flew NORTH to TREPID where light Flak encountered. Silenced gun position in dunes SOUTH of LE TOUQUET. Abandoned task owing to engine trouble. 9/10ths. Cloud 1,000 feet. Visibility 6/8 miles LE TOUQUET area. Three Tomahawks landed MANSTON 13.55 hours.

6.11.41: A Tomahawk, AH887 (W/Cdr. Butler), took off from Manson at 14.13 hours tasked with Arty/R for two Royal Marine 14" Siege Guns which were to conduct a shoot against St Inglevert aerodrome, France. Close protection was to be provided by two more Tomahawks, AH857 (F/O Fleming) and AH893 (F/O Dawson), which took off from Manston at the same time. Fighter escort for the Tomahawks was provided by the Spitfire VB's of the Kenly Wing, No.452 (RAAF), No.485 (RNZAF) and 602 Squadrons.

The Composite Rhubarb Report for his operation is reproduced below verbatim:

6 AIR LIAISON SECTION

No. 26 A.C. Squadron, R.A.F.
APPENDIX "E" TO WAR DIARY, NOVEMBER, 1941.

Composite "RHUBARB" Report.

6.11.41. One Tomahawk, W/Cmdr. Butler 26 Squadron, left Manston 14.13 hours 6/1//41 on Arty/R to observe for two 14" Guns R.M. Siege Regt. Ranging at ST. INGLEVERT aerodrome 785705 ref map O.S. 1/50,000 sheet 38. Two Tomahawks F/O. Fleming and F/O. Dawson left Manston 14.13 hours as close escort, fighter protection being provided by 452, 485 and 602 Squadrons. R.V. made at 1,000 feet over MANSTON with fighter wing 14.15 hours. After testing out crossed coast at DOVER at 3,000 feet at 14.25 hours. On arriving 5 miles off CAP GRIZ NEZ at 9,000 feet target was obscured by cloud. Aircraft dropped to 6,000 feet and shoot commenced at 14.40 hours. First round fell in open ground 800 yards from centre of target at 11 o'clock. Second round unobserved but believed to be about a thousand yards from target at 2 o'clock. Third round unobserved owing to cloud obscuring target and decided to abandon shoot. W/Cmdr. Butler was at once attacked from the stern by one M.E.109 and took violent evasive action before returning to base. F/O. Dawson reports the combat over the FRENCH coast at about 15,000 ft, about 12 aircraft taking part at 14.40 hours. One pilot (unidentified) seemed to bail out from 4,000 feet into sea off CALAIS at 14.55 hours. About 14.50 hours F/O. Dawson saw 4 Spitfires chasing one M.E.109 at 0 ft. towards CALAIS. Having warned W/Cmdr. Butler that M.E.109 was attacking, F/O. Dawson lost both aircraft in cloud. On coming out of cloud at 5,000 feet saw combat taking place between about 6 aircraft at 4,000 ft.
Weather 5/10ths to 6/10ths. Cloud at 6,000 feet over FRENCH coast, visibility 15 – 20 miles. Three aircraft LANDED MANSTON between 15.07 hours and 15.15 hours. Enemy casualties NIL. Own casualties Cat. 2.

No.452 RAAF Squadron records state that in the ensuing battle with the German fighters No.452 Squadron shot down one FW.190 and 2 Me.109F's, damaging three other Me.109F's. On the debit side the Kenly wing lost two Spitfires and one of the No.26 Squadron Tomahawks was damaged by a Me.109.

10.11.41: Two Tomahawks, AH749 (S/Ldr. Hadfield) and AH893 (F/Lt. Wheller), took off from Gatwick at 13.55 hours on a photographic reconnaissance mission of the beaches to the North of Le Touquet. The mission was aborted due to adverse weather and the aircraft returned to Gatwick, landing at 14.20 hours.

21.11.41: There were no operational missions flown again until 21 November when two Tomahawks, AH791 (F/Lt. Rhind) and AH755 (F/O Dawson), attempted a photographic reconnaissance of the beaches in the area Hardelot – Pointe de Lornel. The aircraft took off from Gatwick at 13.17 hours, but aborted due to unsuitable weather (10/10ths cloud at 100 ft) when near Ashford, Kent at 13.35 hours. On the return to base the aircraft got separated; AH755 (F/O Dawson) landed at Gatwick at 13.56, but AH791 (F/Lt. Rhind) force landed at Binney Farm. The pilot was not injured, but the aircraft suffered Category 2 damage.

23.11.41: Two Tomahawks, AH770 (F/Lt. Rhind) and AH749 (P/O Baird), took off from Manston at 11.06 hours on an offensive photographic reconnaissance of the beaches in the Hardelot – Pointe de Lornel area.

The Composite Rhubarb Report for his operation is reproduced below verbatim:

6 AIR LIAISON SECTION

No. 26 A.C. Squadron, R.A.F.
APPENDIX "H" TO WAR DIARY, NOVEMBER, 1941.

Composite "RHUBARB" Report.

23.11.41. Two Tomahawks, F/Lt. Rhind and P/O Baird, 26 Squadron, left MANSTON 11.06 hours on offensive Photo/Recce of beaches HARDELOT – POINTE DE LORNEL. Crossed coast at DUNGENESS at 0 ft at 11.15 hours. About 7 miles off FRENCH coast aircraft separated. F/Lt. Rhind crossed PLAGE ST. CECILY at 0 ft about 11.25 hours. Flew about 2 miles inland before turning NORTH. Ground mist handicapped navigation and photography. Came out SOUTH of Boulogne from whence intense Flak experienced. Opened fire on Flak position but result unobserved. P/O Baird was preparing to photograph coast (believed to be about 3 miles NORTH of BERCK) from sea, when one M.E.109F attacked from starboard bow. P/O Baird orbited and chased E/A firing short burst. Engagement broken off on crossing coast owing to light Flak.

Weather 10/10ths. Cloud 3,000 feet on FRENCH side of channel. Visibility poor. Fair in mid-channel. Both aircraft landed MANSTON 11.55 hours.

24.11.41: Two Tomahawks, AH749 (S/Ldr. Hadfield) and AH773 (P/O Baring), took off from Manston at 11.45 hours. The pair was tasked with conducting an offensive photographic reconnaissance of the beaches in the area Hardelot – Pointe de Lornel.

The Composite Rhubarb reports for this operation are reproduced below verbatim: Note: There were no less than three separate reports submitted for this mission, each contradicting the others in some respect or other.

6 AIR LIAISON SECTION

No. 26 A.C. Squadron, R.A.F.
APPENDIX "J" TO WAR DIARY, NOVEMBER, 1941.

Composite "RHUBARB" Report.

24.11.41. Two Tomahawks, S/Ldr. Hadfield and P/O Baring, 26 Squadron, left MANSTON 11.45 hours on offensive Photo/Recce of beaches HARDELOT – POINTE DE LORNEL. Crossed coast at DUNGENESS at 11.55 hours and made landfall about 2 miles SOUTH of LE TOUQUET at 0 ft. Flew 4 miles inland before turning NORTH round ETAPLES at about 500 feet. S/Ldr. Hadfield made frontal attack firing two one second bursts on a bi-plane training aircraft 3 miles NORTH of ETAPLES but no results observed. Flew North about 2 miles inland from coast when warning of E/A received from P/O Baring. Crossed coast SOUTH of HARDELOT. Saw P/O Baring go down into sea about 15 miles WEST of AMLETEUSE. Aircraft overturned and P/O Baring was seen to swim clear. Whilst orbiting S/Ldr. Hadfield saw 2 M.E.109F's dive on P/O. Baring. He attacked and endeavoured to lead E/A away. S/Ldr. Hadfield was trying to attract attention of two Naval Patrol Vessels off DUNGENESS which both E/A also attacked. S/Ldr. Hadfield landed MANSTON 12.45 hours. 10/10ths cloud 1,500 to 2,000 feet. in channel. Visibility 12 – 15 miles. Own casualties:- One Tomahawk Cat. 3. P/O Baring missing. Enemy casualties NIL,.

Add to Composite RHUBARB Report 26/R/22 dated 24/11. P/O Baring followed S/Ldr Hadfield and fired one 1 second burst at bi-plane trainer (Believed to be F.W.44) from 100 feet. Fire seen entering fuselage and E/A went into steep glide. Engine then developed symptoms of a big-end trouble and pilot immediately turned for home after warning S/Ldr. Hadsfield. P/O Baring was forced down in the sea 10 – 15 miles WEST of AMBLETEUSE at 12.25 hours and was picked up uninjured by a Naval launch at 14.20 hours. Naval personnel reported that one of the M.E.109F's engaged by S/Ldr. Hadfield broke off combat with black smoke pouring from it. Amend casualties to read:- Own 1 Tomahawk Cat.3. P/O. Baring safe. Enemy:- One F.W.44 damaged. One M.E. 109F Damaged.

Ref: Composite RHUBARB report 26/R/22 dated 24.11.41. Pilots further report. Peasant's beach combing on shore NORTH of MERLIMONT PLAGE. Single line of wire only observed and defence posts on dunes did not appear to be manned. Factory ¾ mile SOUTH of Dannes 672377 seen to be in full operation. Nissan type huts and soldiers observed in yards. Type of factory unknown. No defence posts observed in sand dunes between PLAGE AT CECILY and HARDELOT.

R. GENERAL REPORT.

Two Tomahawks, S/Ldr Hadfield and P/O. Baring left MANSTON at 11.45 hours on offensive Photo/Recce beaches HARDELOT – POINTE DE LORNEL. Landfall was made SOUTH of LE TOUQUET both aircraft flying some 4 mile inland before turning NORTH thereby circuiting ETAPLES. S/Ldr carried out a beam attack, opening fire at 200 yards on an F.W. 44 trainer giving a two second burst, but no results observed. P/O Baring made an attack from the port bow opening at 50 yards firing a one second burst. Observed tracer hitting E/A. E/A was seen to judder and went into a steep dive or glide towards the ground both pilots then continued with the recce.

During the photo run P.O Baring's machine developed engine trouble. He informed the S/Ldr and both pilots headed for home, crossing the coast at HARDELOT. P/O Baring was forced down into sea about 15 miles WEST of AMBLETEUSE. S/Ldr Hadfield was circuiting P/O Baring and saw him swim clear of his machine which sank after about 30 seconds. Whilst circling S/Ldr Hadfield saw two M.E.109F's diving from cloud base, one straight at the pilot in the water, the other circled at about 300 feet. S/Ldr Hadfield attacked second E/A making a beam attack, opening at 200 yards firing a 2 second burst. Both aircraft then reformed and followed S/Ldr. Hadfield who was endeavouring to lead them away from P/O Baring. The leading E/A attacked S/Ldr Hadfield who took evasive action by doing a steep turn to port when he saw E/A open fire. As a result of this turn S/Ldr. Hadfield got a second E/A in his sights and made a beam attack opening 200 to 100 yards, giving a 2 second burst. E/A did a sharp turn to starboard but S/Ldr Hadfield was unable to follow as the first E/A was on his tail again. S/Ldr. Hadfield knew his machine to have been hit and turned towards two motor launches he had previously observed. Both E/A followed him, one of them diving towards one of the motor launches. The S/Ldr found his aircraft to be alright and turned round to attack the other E/A. This E/A then made of in the direction of FRANCE. The S/Ldr then returned to base. One of the motor launches picked up P/O Baring two hours later. One member stated he saw black smoke coming from one of the M.E.109's as it broke off the encounter. P/O Baring was landed at DOVER uninjured.

This operation cost the Squadron one Tomahawk slightly damaged and one Tomahawk lost.

27.11.41: This was 26 Squadrons busiest operational day while operating with Tomahawks; two separate operations, each consisting of five aircraft, being flown. The first operation commenced at 10.26 hours when Tomahawks AH857 (F/O Dawson) and AH896 (P/O Baird) took off from Manston on a photographic reconnaissance of the beaches in the Hardelot – Pointe de Lornel area. Three more Tomahawks, AH800 (F/Lt. Wheller), AH791 F/Lt. Rhind) and AH790 (P/O Greville), were tasked with providing close escort; these aircraft also taking off at 10.26 hours. When mid-Channel the mission was aborted due to lack of cloud cover over the French coast and all five aircraft returned to Manston, landing at 11.01 hours.

The second operation of the day commenced at 14.30 when two Tomahawks, AH896 (P/O Baird) and AH857 (F/O Dawson), took off from Manston to attempt the same mission as the one aborted that morning. As with the morning operation, three Tomahawks, AH800 (F/Lt. Wheller), AH791 F/Lt. Rhind) and AH790 (P/O Greville), were tasked with providing close escort; these aircraft also taking off at 14.30 hours. When 20 miles out from the coast the mission was aborted; again due to lack of cloud cover, all five aircraft then landed at Manston at 15.07.

The month of December was a washout for 26 Squadron as far as operational missions were concerned. Only 2 Rhubarbs were attempted on the 9th and 15th of the month. On the first of these, two Tomahawks flown by F/Lt. Wheller and P/O Baird took off from Manston at 11.26 am on 9 December. Their task was to conduct a photographic reconnaissance of the Hardelot – Pointe de Lornel areas, but the mission was aborted when 4 miles off the coast at Hardelot due to unfavourable weather conditions. The aircraft returned, but, both reporting oil trouble, diverted to Detling, Kent, where they landed at 12.45.

The Operation on the 15th of the month commenced when two Tomahawks flown by F/Lt. Rhind and P/O Baring took off from Manston for a photographic reconnaissance of the beaches from Hardelot to Pointe de Lornel. This mission was aborted mid-Channel due to unfavourable weather conditions; both aircraft landing at Manston at 11.02.

4.1.42: Two Tomahawks flown by P/O Dawson and P/O Baird took off from Gatwick at 14.08 hours to photograph the beaches from Hardelot to Pointe de Lornel. The aircraft completed the mission and returned home, crossing the English coast at Eastbourne at 15.00 hours, landing at Gatwick at 15.20.

5.1.42: Two Tomahawks flown by F/O Dawson and P/O Baird took off from Gatwick at 13.33 hours with the same task the previous day. The aircraft reached the Hardelot area at 14.00 hours and the photographic runs were conducted at 600/700 feet. When the Tomahawks were coming out from the Le Touquet estuary they saw six single-engine aircraft, which they could not identify, flying in a northward course over the French coast at an altitude of 1,000 ft. They pilots reported that these aircraft "appeared to follow halfway across the Channel, but no engagement took place". The Tomahawks landed at Gatwick at 15.35.

9.1.42: Two Tomahawks flown by F/Lt. Rhind and F/O Dawson departed Gatwick at 11.47 hours to conduct an offensive photographic reconnaissance of the beaches from Boulogne to Pointe de Lornel. The aircraft crossed the French coast at Hardelot around 12.20; the photo runs being conducted from altitudes of 400 to 500 ft. The aircraft were subjected to "ineffective" light anti-aircraft fire from a point on the north bank of the river Canches. The aircraft returned to Gatwick where they landed at 12.50.

22.1.42: Three Tomahawks flown by F/O Baird, F/Lt. Wheller and F/Lt. Rhind took off from Gatwick at 15.07 hours; tasked with conducting a photographic reconnaissance of the Foret de Hardelot and Neufchatel areas. The aircraft crossed the French coast one mile south of Boulogne Alprech airfield. One Tomahawk strafed a coast gun position on the cliffs. A strafing attack was conducted on a power station one mile south east of Outreau, the aircraft being subjected to light anti-aircraft fire, forcing evasive action by turning sharply to port, exiting over Boulogne Alprech airfield. The aircraft re-crossed the coast heading home with light anti-aircraft fire continuing until they were about two miles out to sea. Few photographs were taken during the mission, which ended when the aircraft landed at Gatwick at 16.06 hours.

This was the last operational mission 26 Squadron conducted with Tomahawks as it was in the process of re-equipping with the more capable North American Mustang fighter, which in several variants would become the standard Army Co-Operation aircraft in RAF service for the remaining years of the war.

4

268 ARMY CO-OPERATION SQUADRON TOMAHAWK OPERATIONS - RHUBARBS OVER HOLLAND AND FIGHTER ESCORT

No.268 Squadron reformed at Bury St. Edmunds with Westland Lysander's as an Army Co-Operation Squadron on 30 September 1940. In October that year 'A' Flight of No.II (2 AC) Squadron was absorbed along with 'B' Flight of No.26 Squadron. No.268 Squadrons Lysander's were used to fly anti-invasion patrols along the south-east coast of England, particularly off East Anglia. Tomahawks began to arrive in May 1941; the Squadron flying Rhubarb operations over Holland and convoy patrols from October that year.

No.268 Squadron commenced operations on 19 October 1941 when two Tomahawks, W/Cdr. Anderson DFC and F/Lt. Aitkens were flown from Snailwell to Coltishall to conduct a Rhubarb operation over the continent. The aircraft departed and crossed the Norfolk coast at 15.00 hours, reaching Ymoiden (probably Ijmuiden) on the Dutch coast forty minutes later, attacking costal targets between Ymoiden (Ijmuiden) and Van Helder over a 20 minute period before turning for home, landing at Coltishall after 1 hour and 40 minutes in the air.

On 1 November two Tomahawks flew to Coltisahall from where they were to fly a Rhubarb operation, but this was cancelled due to unfavorable weather. On the 2nd two Tomahawks took off from Coltishall on Rhubarb, but turned back when off the Dutch coast due to lack of cloud cover. On the 3rd two Tomahawks took off on a Rhubarb from Coltishall, but aborted after sighting the Dutch coast. On 4 November 2 Tomahawks took off from Coltishall on a Rhubarb; it being unclear if the Rhubarb was successfully carried out. What is known is that one of the Tomahawks, flown by F/Lt. Mason, force landed at Horsham St Faith; the aircraft having experiencing "generator drive problems". The following day the Squadron reported only two Tomahawks serviceable.

Top: Tomahawk I AH679 at Bacombe Down. This aircraft later served with No.268 Squadron and No.1686 Bomber (Defence) Training Flight in 1943. MAP
Above: Tomahawks augmented the Westland Lysander in Army Co-Operation Command; often both types equipping different flights or sections of the same squadrons; 268 being one such squadron so equipped. RAF

Two Tomahawks were sent to Coltishall, on the 12th, but planned operations were cancelled on the 12, 13 and 14th. Unfortunately squadron records for the rest of November are hand written and difficult to decipher. However, correlation with other operational records concludes that it is unlikely that any further Rhubarb sorties were flown during the month.

On 16 December 1941, three Tomahawks, flown by W/Cdr. Anderson, F/Lt. Mason and P/O Griffin, took off at 14.00 hours and flew to Ibsley on detachment to No.501 Squadron; a ground party had left for Ibsley at 08.00 that morning. During the course of the detachment, which ended on 21 December when the three Tomahawks returned to Snailwell, the three pilots each flew one convoy patrol of 2 hours 45 minutes, and section attacks were practiced between 2 Tomahawks and 2 No.501 Squadron Spitfires, as well as individual mock dogfights between Spitfires and Tomahawks.

On 17 January 1942, two Tomahawks, flown by F/Lt. Clapin and P/O Griffin, flew to Ibsley for another detachment to No.501 Squadron, with each pilot flying a half hour convoy patrol. A detachment of three Tomahawks was to go to Ibsley on the 19th for operations with 501 Squadron, but this was cancelled due to weather until the following day when it was again cancelled, this time for two weeks; the detachment eventually taking place on 11 February when two Tomahawks flown by P/O Griffin and P/O Gray took off for Ibsley at 16.00 hours. When landing, P/O Gray crashed, leaving only one Tomahawk operational. The following day a Tomahawk flown by F/Lt. Clapin took off for Ibsley at 11.00 hours followed at 14.00 hours by a Lysander flown by P/O Hawkins. The Tomahawk was to replace the one lost when P/O Gray crashed the previous day. The other Tomahawk, flown to Ibsley by P/O Griffin the previous day, was reported unserviceable as it had "sheared its main drive". The following day P/O Griffin returned to Snailwell by air to collect and fly another Tomahawk to Ibsley, where he arrived again in the afternoon. There were now four pilots, four Tomahawks and one Lysander at Ibsley. The flap that emerged when it became clear that the German Battlecruisers *Scharnhorst* and *Gneisenau* were conducting their legendary 'Channel dash' was to fly over the 268 Squadron detachments at Ibsley due to "un-serviceability of aircraft".

On the 14th F/Lt. Clapin and P/O Hawkins returned to Snailwell by air. P/O Griffin, flying a, Tomahawk, conducted a convoy patrol in company with 2 Spitfires of 501 Squadron on the 14th; another patrol, lasting 1 hour and 20 minutes, with a Tomahawk and six 501 Squadron Spitfires, being flown on the 16th. On the 17th, six Spitfire VB's of 501 Squadron and a single Tomahawk flown by P/O Griffin were ordered off the ground to intercept enemy raiders; none being encountered, the aircraft subsequently landing after a patrol of 1 hour and 5 minutes.

On the 18th, a Tomahawk flown by P/O Griffin took off in company with six Spitfire VB's from 501 Squadron; the Flight being tasked with providing cover for a Rhubarb operation flown by another squadron. The Spitfires and

Tomahawk flew to an area 4 miles off Pointe de Barfleur (Cherbourg) where they rendezvoused with the four Spitfires that were conducting an attack on a distillery at Baupte, Normandy, all ten Spitfires and the Tomahawk then returning to base having encountered no enemy aircraft during the mission.

Two Tomahawks and four Spitfires from 501 Squadron took off from Ibsley at 14.45 hours on 21 February; the Flight being tasked to look for ships that had been reported to be around 20 miles south of Swanage. No ships were seen and the Spitfires and Tomahawks turned for home. The Tomahawks, which were positioned on the port and to the rear of the formation, were weaving when the mixed Flight was attacked by a Section of 2 Spitfires that had been vectored onto the formation which had been mistakenly reported as enemy aircraft. During the firing pass F/O Hawkins Tomahawk was hit in the oil cooler by a 20 mm cannon shell. Although damaged, the Tomahawk was flyable and Hawkins successfully reached the coast, continuing inland for a distance of around 5 miles before his engine stopped and he force landed near Corfe Castle, hitting a tree. The aircraft ended upside down with Hawkins being killed.

Another convoy patrol was flown by F/Lt. Clapin in a Tomahawk in company with two Spitfires from 501 Squadron on 24 February.

One Tomahawk flown by F/O Morris went to Ibsley on 3 March. On 12 March all Tomahawks were grounded for modifications, only one being serviceable by the 15th; this being flown to Ibsley by W/Cdr. Anderson.

On 20 March, S/Ldr. Watson Smyth and F/Lt. Clapin went to the AFDU at Duxford where they received instruction on and flew a North American Mustang. On the 23rd a Tomahawk was delivered from 241 Squadron which was converting to Mustangs. Two other Tomahawks were picked up from 241 Squadron by 268 Squadron pilots.

On 2 April 1942, a report was received that there were some 70 ships of undetermined nationality in an area off the East Anglia coast. Alarm bells rang and aircraft were sent to investigate. Among these were four Tomahawks flown by W/Cdr. Anderson, F/Lt. Mason, F/Lt. Clapin and F/O Morris, which took off at 06.15 and landed at 07.45. Only a small number of British vessels were located and when it was learned that the unidentified ships were actually a British convoy the flap was over.

This impromptu patrol was the Tomahawks swansong in 268 Squadron service, and indeed that of the home based Tomahawk Squadrons; army Co-Op exercises and training flights being conducted as the squadron awaited re-equipment with Mustangs which effectively commenced on 19 April 1942 when an Armstrong Whitworth Whitely took eight 268 Squadron pilots and two from 241 squadron to Speke where 10 Mustangs were collected and flown to Snailwell. From the following day training commenced on Mustangs, although Tomahawks were still used in small numbers during the rest of the month and the first few days of May, some of these aircraft eventually going to No.231 Squadron in Northern Ireland; five being collected on the 29th.

Top: Tomahawks of 268 Squadron flew mixed formation patrols with Spitfire VB's of No.501 Squadron, similar to this VB operating with the AFDU at Duxford. RAF Above: As with many Army Co-Operation Squadrons, No.268 replaced its Tomahawks with the more capable North American Mustang I. This Mustang IA, FD449, is as at Air Services Training Ltd, Hamble, Hampshire awaiting delivery to No.268 Squadron.

5

400 RCAF ARMY CO-OPERATION SQUADRON - RHUBARB AND POPULAR OPERATIONS OVER FRANCE

No.400 Squadron RCAF was initially formed as No.10 Army Co-Operation Squadron in 1932. It was renumbered No-110 'City of Toronto' Army Co-Op Squadron on 15 November 1937. Called to active service at the outbreak of World War II, it moved to the United Kingdom where it was renumbered 400 RCAF Army Co-Op Squadron on 2 March 1941, equipped with Westland Lysander's and Curtiss Tomahawks at RAF Odiham, Hampshire.

In preparation for Tomahawk operations W/Cdr. MaKay and four other pilots went to Old Sarum on 1 March 1941 for a course on Tomahawks. The Squadron being officially re-designated No.400 on the 2nd and not the 1st of the month as is often stated.

Although not operational, the Squadrons first casualties as a result of enemy action occurred on the night of 16.17 April 1941 when the London area was heavily attacked by German bombers, 400 Squadron suffering I killed and I seriously injured.

By 30 April 400 Squadron had 7 Tomahawks on strength and all squadron pilots had completed the Tomahawk conversion course. The Squadron continued to operate Lysander's, un-serviceability of which was very high.

Throughout the summer and autumn months the squadron worked up on the Tomahawk, and, like other Army Co-Operation Squadrons was heavily involved in the endless cycle of Army exercises. Other training included air to air affiliation exercises such as that conducted on 31 October 1941 when Tomahawks conducted mock attacks on Beauforts of No.415 Squadron.

In early November 1941 the squadron commenced 'Rhubarb' and 'Popular' operations over the continent; 'Popular', being basically a Rhubarb by another name. Squadron and supporting Command operational records are incomplete and in many cases unclear and or contradictory in regards to distinguishing between operational and training sorties.

Operational Rhubarbs by 400 Squadron commenced on 5 November 1941 when two Tomahawks flown by W/Cdr. Kerby and P/O Jackson flew to Tangmere. One of the Tomahawks was declared U/S due to a minor defect and the Rhubarb was cancelled. The Rhubarb was flown the following day with the same two pilots; the Tomahawks tasked with conducting a photographic reconnaissance of Le Cayeux, Dieppe, France. The D/F equipment sent to Beachy Head on 31 October in preparation for the Squadrons commencement of Rhubarb operations was reported to be working.

8.11.41: Planned Rhubarb cancelled due to lack of cloud cover over the target area. The Squadron lost Tomahawk AH845, which ditched in water during a non-operational low flying gunnery practice over Chesil Beach near to Lyme Regis.

10.11.41: Two Tomahawks flown by S/Ldr. Wendell and P/O McGraph took off on a Rhubarb over France, but the mission was aborted mid-Channel as Luftwaffe fighters had been reported over the French coast.

11.11.41: The Rhubarb aborted the previous day was flown in the late afternoon, the two Tomahawks returning to Tangmere where they remained overnight as darkness closed in.

12.11.41: The Rhubarb planned for this date was cancelled due to unfavourable weather. The squadrons records show that on this date orders were issued that in telephone conversations Rhubarbs were to be referred to as "Martian".

21.11.41: There was an air raid warning sounded at Odiham; a single German aircraft flying over the station around 15,000 ft.

22.11.41: Two Tomahawks flown by F/Lt. Morris and P/O Rogers took off on a Rhubarb in the afternoon. The mission was completed and the aircraft returned to Tangmere "without untoward incident".

24.11.41: A Rhubarb operation was attempted, but aborted due to unfavourable weather.

25.11.41: Two Tomahawks took off on a Rhubarb operation over Le Treport, France, but the pilots, F/Lt. Woods and F/Lt. Ogilvie, aborted the mission due to weather.

27.11.41: Two Tomahawks flown by F/Lt. Norris and P/O Knight took off on a Rhubarb operation over Le Havre, France. The aircraft were subjected to light anti-aircraft fire and a Me.109 fighter was noted at 2,000 ft, the Tomahawks losing the German fighter in a climb.

Poor weather on the last two days of November grounded all squadron aircraft. On the 29th the squadron had four Lysander's and 15 Tomahawks serviceable. The squadron Tiger Moth was also unserviceable.

5.12.41: Four Tomahawks took off on a Rhubarb, but were recalled by control while en-route as the Luftwaffe was mounting a "standing patrol over the target area".

6.12.41: Four Tomahawks were sent to Manston from where they were to fly a Rhubarb. Only two of the Tomahawks, flown by F/Lt. Ogilvie and P/O Peters, flew the Rhubarb; photographing bomb damage to a distillery at Beauchamps.

11.12.41: Two Tomahawks took off on a "Popular" operation, but owing to lack of cloud cover over the French coast the pilots, F/Lt. Norris and P/O Hall, aborted the mission and returned to base.

12.12.41: Two Tomahawks flown by F/Lt. Norris and P/O Bissky, conducted a "Popular" operation, photographing the Berck Plage and Le Touquet areas. The squadron records state that the Tomahawks "exchanged fire with enemy gunboats".

13.12.41: Two Tomahawks, P/O Jackson and P/O English, took off from Manston on a "Popular" operation at 10.30 hours. On the return flight a radio transmission was received as follows:-
"11.05 hours S.16 (Jackson) 'Vector' Subway 4 '305 Degrees'
"11.06 hours S.18 (English) 'Hey on your tail' S.16 (Jackson) 'I'll take care of this baby.'" Following this transmission nothing else was heard from either aircraft, which were reported as overdue at 13.30 hours. Fighter Command Intelligence reported that an "intercepted message from a German patrol reported two aircraft dived into sea approximately 12 miles off Etaples at time of lost contact". The position agreed with approximate position given by the direction finder at Beachy Head. Radio location also reported interceptions from German aircraft in the area at the time and it quickly became clear that the two Tomahawks had been shot down by German fighters and the pilots were reported as missing at 16.00 hours that afternoon. German records show the Tomahawks being shot down by Me.109F's of 4/JG 2 (Ltn. Karl Rees) at 12.09 hours and 6//JG 2 (Uffz Gerhard Heinz) at 12.15 respectively.

15.12.41: a "Popular" operation was flown by two Tomahawks, P/O McGrath and P/O Rogers. A second "Popular" operation, F/Lt. Woods and P/O Gordon, was aborted due to a lack of cloud cover.

16.12.41: Two Tomahawks, F/Lt. Woods and P/O Gordon, flew a "Popular" operation. The target area was the coast south of Le Treport, but navigation problems and "enemy ground interference", assumed to be anti-aircraft fire, forced the aircraft to turn north where they photographed the coast area to the south of Ber-sur-mer. The aircraft flown by P/O Gordon landed with a bullet hole in the rudder.

21.12.41: Two Tomahawks took off on a "Popular" operation, but returned owing to weather.

27.12.41: Two Tomahawks took off on a "Popular" operation, but aborted when 8 miles from French coast due to lack of cloud cover.

28.12.41: Two Tomahawks attempted a "Popular" operation, but this was aborted due to weather.

4.1.42: Two Tomahawks, P/O Peters and P/O Clarke, took off on a "Popular" operation and photographed areas between Le Touquet and Berck-Sur-Mer "with oblique's from 200-300 ft", following which they returned to Le Touquet and strafed the aerodrome, road transport and some barges. The aircraft reported light anti-aircraft fire.

These were the last two operational sorties 400 Squadron would fly in Tomahawks, which continued to be used for training until the Squadron re-equipped with Mustangs in the summer months.

6

TOMAHAWK SQUADRONS ON THE HOME FRONT 1941-43

In addition to No.403 (RCAF), 26, 268 and 400 (RCAF) Squadrons, no less than nine other squadrons operated Tomahawks on the home front.

No.II Army Co-Operation Squadron

No.II (AC) Squadron began to replace its Lysander's with Tomahawks' which were used for training before the squadron converted to Mustangs in April 1942. There are many unofficial references to No.II Squadron flying operational Tomahawk sorties over France in late 1941 and early 1942. However, no operational records such as Form 540/541, Composite Rhubarb Reports or other Squadron or Command records show any such missions being flown. The squadron, like most home based Tomahawk squadrons, was heavily involved in Army Co-Operation exercises, the details of which often read like real operations in RAF documents.

Preparations for receipt of Tomahawks started on 23 May 1941 when a wireless set was sent to Henlow to be fitted to a Tomahawk. In early June, plans were set out for an extension of the landing strip at Sawbridgeworth so it could accommodate the use of Tomahawks. On 26 June, the Squadron Commanding Officer and two other pilots went to Old Sarum for a conversion course on Tomahawks. Three more pilots commenced Tomahawk conversion on 3 July. Throughout July and August the squadron continued to operate Lysander's while some pilots continued conversion training on Tomahawks, which was completed by all but three pilots by 20 August, and the first two Tomahawks were collected from Messrs Cunliffe Owen Aircraft Co. Ltd. on the 22nd; two more being collected on the 24th.

On 20 April 1942 four Mustangs were collected from Speke; 6 more being collected the following day. From then the squadron took on more of a Mustang flavour, but continued operating Tomahawks for a short period.

No.613 Squadron operated Tomahawk I/IIA/IIB's from Doncaster, Yorkshire. This Tomahawk IIB, AK162/SY-N, is in flight over Auckley Common to the east of Doncaster in 1942. MOI

No.168 Squadron

No.168 Squadron formed from an element of 268 Squadron on 15 June 1942. The squadron was equipped with Tomahawks which were replaced by Mustangs in November that year.

No.171 Squadron

No.171 Squadron formed as an Army Co-Operation/tactical reconnaissance squadron at Gatwick on 15 June 1942. The squadron was equipped with Tomahawks for a short period only as they were replaced by North American Mustangs in October that year.

231 Squadron

No.231 Squadron reformed as an Army Co-Operation Squadron on 1 July 1940, at Aldergrove, Northern Ireland, operating Westland Lysander's; conversion to Tomahawks commencing in September 1941, these being operated alongside Lysander's. A detachment of Lysander's remained in Ulster when the squadron moved to Yorkshire in March 1943, conversion to Mustangs taking place in April that year; the Lysander detachment operating until July.

No.239 Squadron

No.239 Squadron was reformed as an Army Co-Operation Squadron in September 1940. Initially equipped with Westland Lysander's it eventually received some Tomahawk's in summer 1941, some Hurricanes also apparently being received, before it was re-equipped with Mustangs in early summer 1942. No operational sorties were flown with Tomahawks.

No.241 Squadron

No.241 Squadron was reformed from a Flight of No.614 Squadron at Inverness, Scotland, on 25 September 1940. The squadron was to be equipped with Lysander's, but also received a few Blackburn Rocs, which were used for dive bombing trials. From March 1942, Tomahawks began to replaced the Lysander's, these being used for tactical reconnaissance training before the squadron converted to Hawker Hurricanes, moving to North Africa in April 1942.

No.414 RCAF Squadron

No.414 Squadron RCAF formed as an Army Co-Operation Squadron at Croydon on 3 August 1941, equipped with Lysander and later Tomahawk fighters.

No.430 RCAF Squadron

No.430 Squadron RCAF formed on 1 January 1943 as an Army Co-Operation Squadron. It was equipped with Tomahawks for a short period, receiving Mustang I's before the squadron commenced operational flying.

No. 613 Squadron

No.613 Royal Auxiliary Air Force Squadron formed at Ringway on 1 March 1939. The squadron was equipped with Hawker Hinds before converting to

Hawker Hectors in November 1939, with Westland Lysander's being received from April 1940. The Hectors and Lysander were used on operations over France during the German advance into France and the Low Countries in May 1940.

From August 1941, Tomahawks began to arrive; these being used for tactical reconnaissance training before the squadron converted to North American Mustangs in April 1942; operational flying commencing in December that year.

In addition to the above mentioned squadron several other units operated Tomahawks in small numbers on trials and other duties; for example No.1686 Bomber (Defence) Training Flight. The Tomahawk was also extensively operated by British and Commonwealth units in other theatres including North Africa and the Canadian Home Defence Squadrons.

The Tomahawk's career as an operational fighter with home based squadrons was relatively short lived with only the MK.I and MK.IIA being used operationally. However, the Tomahawk MK.IIB was used operationally in other theatres, notably the Middle East and North Africa, alongside later variants of the P-40 which were named Kittyhawk in British and Commonwealth service. RAF Fitters test run the Alison V-1710-33 engine of Tomahawk IIB, AK326, in the hands of No.107 Maintenance Unit located at Kasfareet, Egypt. RAF

APPENDICES

Appendix I

P-40B Specification – equivalent in most respects to the Tomahawk I

Information taken from Curtiss Report No.8302 and Memorandum Report Serial No.PHQ-M-19-1227-A

Level Flight Speeds at Design Altitude of 15,000 ft. with Actual Gross Weight of 6,833 lb.

Maximum speed   347 m.p.h. at 3000 r.p.m. with 1050 b.hp. (113% rated)
High Speed   332 m.p.h. at 2600 r.p.m. with 920 b.hp. (99% rated)
Operating Speed 306 m.p.h. at 2280 r.p.m. with 698 b.hp. (75% rated)
Cruising Speed   202 m.p.h. at 1950 r.p.m. with 322 b.hp. (35% rated)

Optimum Range and Endurance with 120 gal fuel and no bombs.

At High Speed 430 miles at 3.6 mi./gal. or 1.3 hrs. at 92 gal./hr.
At Operating Speed 620 miles at 5.2 mi./gal. or 2.0 hrs. at 59 gal./hr.
At Min Cruise Speed 1,010 miles at 8.4 mi./gal. or 5.0 hrs. at 24 gal/hr.

Practical Range and Endurance with 120 gal. fuel and no bombs.

At Operating Speed 495 miles at 4.1 mi./gal. or 1.6 hrs. at 74 gal./hr.
At Min Cruising Speed 805 miles at 6.7 mi./gal. or 4.0 hrs. at 30 gal./hr.

Climb Data with Gross Weight of 6,833 lb.

Standard Altitude ft.	S/L	5000	10000	15000	25000	32400
Climbing Speed m.p.h.	143	143	143	139	126	
Engine Speed r.p.m.	3000	3000	3000	2600	2600	2600
Total Power b.hp.	952	1002	1050	835	585	
Maximum rate f.p.m.	2900	2985	3070	2160	935	100
Minimum Time min.	0	1.7	3.35	5.11	12.0	32.0

Ceiling:

Normal Engine Operation: Service Ceiling 32,400 ft. Absolute Ceiling 33,300 ft.

Wing Loading: 28.9 lb./sq. ft.
Wing Area: 236 sq. ft.
Wing Span: 37 ft 3.5 in
Aspect Ratio: 5.9
Wing Type: L.W. Monoplane
High Lift Devices: Split Flaps
Landing Gear Type: Retractable
Crew: 1

Engine

Number	1
Manufacturer	Allison
Spec. No.	Vee
Model	V-1710-33
No. Cyl.	12
Supercharger Blower Ratios	8.77:1
Turbo Type	None
Prop. Gear Ratio	2:1
Compression Ratio	6.65:1
Cooling	Liquid
Carburetor Type	PT-13E1
Setting	AC.110
Fuel	100 octane
Intake Type	Ramming
Exhaust Type	Individual Short Stacks

Rating:	Altitude ft.	Power b.hp.	Speed r.p.m.	Man. Pr. in Hg	Time Limit Minutes	Blower Ratio	Mixture F/A
Take-Off	S.L	1040	2800	442	5	8.77	Auto Rich
Normal	S.L.	808	2600	35.3			
Normal	12,000	930	2600	35.3			
Military	13,600	1040	3000	40	5		

PROPELLERS

Number 1… Mfr. Curtiss…   Type… Constant Speed…   Rotation R.H.
Diameter   11 ft. 0 in… No of blades 3… Type Control Electric
Setting   24 deg to 49 deg at 42 "… Balde Dwg. No.   89301-3…   Hub Dwg.
No C532D-F24

WEIGHTS AND BALANCE
Performance obtained at Design Gross Wt. – 6,835 lb.

Weight Empty	5,589 lb.
Normal Gross Weight	7,326 lb.
Normal Fuel	120 gal.
Max. Fuel	160 gal.
Fuel Weight	720 lb (120 gal.)
Armament weight	600 lb.
Armouur weight:	93 lb

Appendix II

Tomahawk I/IIA Squadrons in the UK

Squadron	Role
II (2)	Army Co-Operation
26	Army Co-Operation
168	Army Co-Operation
171	Army Co-Operation
231	Army Co-Operation
239	Army Co-Operation
241	Army Co-Operation
268	Army Co-Operation
400 (RCAF)	Army Co-Operation
403 (RCAF)	Fighter Command
414 (RCAF)	Army Co-Operation
430 (RCAF)	Army Co-Operation
613	Army Co-Operation

In addition to the above mentioned squadron several other units operated Tomahawks in small numbers on trials and other duties; for example No.1686 Bomber (Defence) Training Flight. The Tomahawk was also extensively operated by British and Commonwealth units in other theatres including North Africa and the Canadian Home Defence Squadrons.

GLOSSARY

AA	Anti Aircraft
AC	Army Co-Operation
AFDU	Air Fighting Development Unit
BCATP	British Commonwealth Air Training Plan
Cat.	Category
CO	Commanding Officer
Cyl.	Cylinder
DFC	Distinguished Flying Cross
E/A	Enemy Aircraft
F/Lt.	Flight Lieutenant
F/O	Flying Officer
FW	Focke Wulf
GP	General Purpose
HT	High Tension
MAP	Ministry of Aircraft Production
ME	Messerschmitt
MOI	Ministry Of Information
P	Pursuit
P/O	Pilot Officer
RAAF	Royal Australian Air Force
RAF	Royal Air Force
RCAF	Royal Canadian Air Force
RM	Royal Marine
RNZAF	Royal New Zealand Air Force
RV	Rendezvous
SAAF	South African Air Force
S/Ldr.	Squadron Leader
SL	Sea Level
U/S	Unserviceable
USAAC	United States Army Air Corp
W/Cdr.	Wing Commander
XP	Experimental Pursuit

BIBLIOGRAPHY

No.26 Squadron Operations Record Book Form 541 1 -31 October 1941

No.26 Squadron Operations Record Book Form 541 1 -30 November 1941

No.26 Squadron Operations Record Book Form 541 1 -31 December 1941

No.26 Squadron Operations Record Book Form 541 1 -31 January 1942

6 Air Liaison Section Composite Rhubarb Reports for No.26 Squadron 16
October 1941 – 22 January 1942

No.268 Squadron Operations Record Book Form 540 1 February 1941 – 30
June 1942

No.403 (RCAF) Squadron Operations Record Book Form 540 1 March – 31
May 1941

No.400 (RCAF) Squadron Operations Record Book Form 540 1 March 1941 –
30 November 1942

No.II Squadron Operations Record Book Form 540 1 January 1941 – 30
November 1942

Curtiss Report No.8302

Memorandum Report Serial No. PHQ-M-19-1227-A

P-40B (Tomahawk) Manufacturers Performance Summary

P-40B (Tomahawk) Manufacturers Characteristic Summary

In addition many other operational and non-operation documents were
consulted in the preparation of this volume

Note: Many operational records were incomplete and most of the Squadrons
Form 541 was nonexistent due to the Squadrons not being involved in
operational sorties

ABOUT THE AUTHOR

Hugh, a historian and author, has published in excess of thirty books; non-fiction and fiction, writing under his own name as well as utilising two different pseudonyms. He has also written for several international magazines, whist his work has been used as reference for many other projects ranging from the aviation industry, international news corporations, film media to encyclopedias and the computer gaming industry. He currently resides in his native Scotland

Other titles by the Author include

British Battlecruisers of World War 1 – Operational Log, July 1914-June 1915
Hurricane IIB Combat Log – 151 Wing RAF North Russia 1941
RAF Meteor Jet Fighters in World War II, an Operational Log
Typhoon IA/B Combat Log - Operation Jubilee August 1942
Defiant MK.I Combat Log - Fighter Command, May-September 1940
Eurofighter Typhoon – Storm over Europe
Tornado F.2/F.3 Air Defence Variant
Boeing X-36 – Tailless Agility Flight Research Aircraft
X-32 – The Boeing Joint Strike Fighter
X-35 – Progenitor to the F-35 Lightning II
X-45 Uninhabited Combat Air Vehicle
F-84 Thunderjet – Republic Thunder
USAF Jet Powered Fighters – XP-59-XF-85
XF-92 – Convairs Arrow
The Battle Cruiser Fleet at Jutland
Light Battlecruisers and the 2nd Battle of Heligoland Bight
Saab Gripen, The Nordic Myth
American Teens
Dassault Rafale – The Gallic Squall
Boeing F/A-18E/F Super Hornet

www.ingramcontent.com/pod-product-compliance
Lightning Source LLC
LaVergne TN
LVHW061328060426
835511LV00012B/1919